
Take a trip to

EAST GERMANY

Keith Lye

General Editor

Henry Pluckrose

Franklin Watts

London New York Sydney Toronto

Facts about East Germany

Area:
108,178 sq. km.
(41,768 sq. miles)

Population:
16,734,000

Capital:
East Berlin

Largest cities:
East Berlin (1,186,000)
Leipzig (559,000)
Dresden (523,000)
Karl-Marx-Stadt (319,000)
Magdeburg (289,000)

Official language:
German

Religion:
Christianity

Main exports:
Engineering goods, precision instruments, chemicals

Currency:
Mark

Franklin Watts
12a Golden Square
London W1

Franklin Watts Inc.
387 Park Avenue South
New York, N.Y. 10016

ISBN: UK Edition 0 86313 497 1
ISBN: US Edition 0 531 10287 4
Library of Congress Catalog
Card No: 86 50897

Maps: Susan Kinsey and Simon Roulestone
Design: Edward Kinsey
Stamps: Stanley Gibbons
Photographs: J. Allan Cash 17, 21; Paul Forrester 10; Keith Lye 12, 31; Tom Sharman 7, 8, 9, 14, 15, 16, 18, 20, 22, 24, 25, 28, 29; Frank Spooner 19, 23, 30; ZEFA 3, 4, 5, 6, 13, 26, 27
Front Cover: Tim Sharman
Back Cover: Frank Spooner
Typeset by Ace Filmsetting Ltd
Frome, Somerset
Printed in Hong Kong

In 1945, at the end of World War II, the victorious Allies divided Germany into four zones. In 1949, the three western zones merged to form West Germany, while the Russian zone became East Germany. The picture shows Dresden, which has been rebuilt since 1945 when it was in ruins.

Berlin, Germany's capital, was also divided into four zones. The American, British and French zones now form West Berlin. The Russian zone became East Berlin. A wall, built by the East Germans in 1961, separates East and West Berlin.

People can travel between East and West Berlin by passing through frontier posts, called checkpoints. They must produce their passports at these posts. Some people travel on the S-Bahn, an elevated railway, while others go by car or bus.

East Germany is bordered on the north by the Baltic Sea. Separated from the mainland by a narrow channel is the island of Rügen. It has several seaside resorts which are popular during the warm summers.

Most of East Germany consists of a plain broken by low hills and lakes. Neubrandenburg is a town in the North German plain, much of which has less than 640 mm (25 in) of rain per year.

East Germany's southern uplands are wetter and have colder winters than the North German plain. Eisenach in the southwest stands on the edge of a highland region, the Thüringerwald (or Thuringian Forest).

The Erzgebirge (Ore Mountains) rise in the southeast along the border with Czechoslovakia. These mountains, which contain East Germany's highest point at 1,214 m (3,983 ft), can be visited by cable cars.

The picture shows some stamps and money used in East Germany. The main unit of currency is the mark, which is divided into 100 pfennig.

East Germany

DENMARK
Baltic Sea
Rügen
Rostock
Wismar
Neubrandenburg
Schwerin
North German Plain
EAST GERMANY
R. Oder
WEST GERMANY
POLAND
West Berlin
East Berlin
Brandenburg
Potsdam
Magdeburg
R. Elbe
Cottbus
Dessau
R. Neisse
Harz Mtns
Saale R.
Halle
Leipzig
Eisenach
Erfurt
Dresden
Weimar
Gera
Karl-Marx-Stadt
Thüringerwald
Zwickau
Erzgebirge
CZECHOSLOVAKIA

In 1945, the Big Three – the US President Harry Truman, the Russian leader Joseph Stalin, and the British Prime Minister Winston Churchill – met in Potsdam, 26 km (16 miles) southwest of Berlin. Here, in this building, which is now a museum, they discussed the future of Germany.

Under Russian rule, the German Democratic Republic, as East Germany is officially called, became a Communist country. The capital East Berlin has many signs of Russian rule, including this statue of Lenin, the Communist leader of the Russian Revolution in 1917.

Leipzig, East Germany's second largest city, was badly damaged in World War II. It is a major industrial, commercial and cultural city, famed for its international trade fairs. Today, 76 out of every 100 East Germans live in cities or towns.

Protestantism began in Germany. Although East Germany's government disapproves of religion, more than half of the people are Protestants and there are also some Roman Catholics. The Protestant church in this picture is near Dresden.

Agriculture employs one out of every ten workers. The government owns more than 90 percent of the farmland. On co-operative farms, the farmers work together and share the profits. On state farms, the workers receive wages.

Farmland covers 44 percent of East Germany. Leading crops include barley, oats, potatoes, rye, sugar beet and wheat. The picture shows a maize farm in the south, where the land is fertile. Cattle, pigs and sheep are reared in East Germany.

Fishing is an important industry. This picture shows Warnemünde, a fishing port on the Baltic Sea coast. Warnemünde is the outpost of Rostock, an industrial port which lies a few miles from the coast on the banks of the Warnow River.

East Germany is the world's top producer of lignite (brown coal), seen here being loaded on to a train. Lignite is used in the country's many chemical industries. East Germany also mines some coal and potash, which is used to make fertilizers.

East Germany once depended mainly on farming. But with Russia's help, it has become one of the world's top ten manufacturing countries. Among its industrial products are many kinds of transport equipment and vehicles, including farm tractors.

Most industries are government-owned. They employ 50 percent of East Germany's work force. Besides chemicals and transport equipment, the country also makes such things as iron and steel, textiles and ships. This shipyard is in Rostock.

Education is free and compulsory for ten years. Many young children attend a kindergarten, such as this one at Neubrandenburg, before they start their compulsory schooling at the age of six.

After completing their basic education, some children go on to vocational schools. Others enter high schools and prepare for a university education. In 1983, East Germany had 53 universities.

East Germany is one of the most prosperous of Communist countries. Many people in the cities live in apartments. The government provides free medical care, free higher education and various other benefits.

Families enjoy a day out at a summer fair. Popular hot snacks at outdoor events include various kinds of sausage, such as bratwurst and knackwurst. Food is generally cheap and plentiful in East Germany.

Many East Germans enjoy seeing plays or listening to music. Germany has produced many writers, including Johann Wolfgang von Goethe, Germany's leading poet and dramatist, who lived in this house in Weimar.

Some great composers were born in what is now East Germany. Eisenach was the birthplace of Johann Sebastian Bach. Other composers included George Frederick Handel (born in Halle) and Richard Wagner (born in Leipzig).

Germany's historic cities attract tourists. Among Dresden's great buildings is the Zwinger Palace which contains many artistic treasures. This palace, like most of Dresden's buildings, was restored after having been damaged in World War II.

Young people enjoy sports of many kinds. Soccer is the leading team game. Facilities also exist for a wide range of other activities, including track and field events and swimming. East German athletes are prominent in international sport.

Factory sports associations encourage the workers to attend keep fit classes. Every town has a well equipped gymnasium and many other facilities which are open to everyone, free of charge.

Children learn about politics in school and many people join political groups. The picture shows preparations for a political rally in East Berlin. Its aim is to oppose Western military policies and to call for peace.

Index